UNLEASHING THE POWER OF SELF-LOVE

JENNIFER L. BALDWIN

ABOUT THE AUTHOR

Jennifer L. Baldwin, is a passionate advocate for self-love and personal growth. With a deep commitment to helping others discover their true worth and potential, Jennifer Baldwin has dedicated her life to empowering individuals to lead more fulfilling and authentic lives. Through her work as a best-selling author and Master life coach, Jennifer Baldwin has inspired countless people to embark on the transformative journey of self-love. Jennifer Baldwin envisions a world where self-love is the foundation of personal and collective well-being. She is dedicated to continuing her mission of spreading awareness and education about the importance of self-love. Through her writings, speaking engagements, and coaching, Jennifer Baldwin aims to inspire and empower more individuals to embark on the journey of self-love and create positive, lasting change in their lives. To contact the author, visit www.jennbaldwin.com.

Copyright © 2024 Jennifer Baldwin

All rights reserved. No part of this publication may be reproduced, distributed, or transmitted in any form or by any means without the prior written permission of the publisher, except in the case of brief quotations embodied in articles and reviews.

ISBN 979-8-3303-4931-9
Cover Designed and Published by JR Publishing, 2024

Dedication

This book is dedicated to all who are on the journey to find and embrace their true selves. May you discover the courage to love yourself deeply, the strength to always stand in your truth, and the freedom to pursue your dreams unapologetically.

To my family and friends, whose unwavering support and love have been my anchor and guiding light—thank you for believing in me, even when I struggled to believe in myself.

And to anyone who has ever felt lost, alone, or unworthy—this book is for you. May it be a reminder that you are enough, just as you are, and that the most profound love you can ever achieve is the love you give to yourself.

Table of Contents

Introduction 1

Understanding Self-Love 6

The Journey Inward. 13

Cultivating Self-Compassion. 19

Building a Positive Self-Image 26

Nurturing Your Mind, Body, and Soul. 33

Self-Love in Relationships. 41

Living Authentically and Purposefully. 49

Sustaining Self-Love. 57

Introduction: Unleashing the Power of Self-Love

Welcome to a journey that has the potential to transform your life from the inside out. "Unleashing the Power of Self-Love" is not just a book; it's a guide to discovering, embracing, and nurturing the most important relationship you will ever have—the one with yourself. In a world that often emphasizes external achievements and societal approval, cultivating self-love can be a revolutionary act.

Why Self-Love Matters

Self-love is the foundation of a healthy, fulfilling life. It influences every aspect of our existence, from our mental and emotional well-being to our relationships and personal growth. When we love ourselves, we create a solid base from which we can face challenges, pursue our passions, and build meaningful connections with others.

In our busy lives, it's easy to neglect self-love. We often prioritize work, family, and social obligations over our own needs. We may struggle with negative self-talk, self-doubt, and feelings of unworthiness.

This book aims to shift that focus, guiding you toward a more compassionate, accepting, and empowered relationship with yourself.

The Journey Ahead

In "Unleashing the Power of Self-Love," we will explore various aspects of self-love, providing practical strategies, insights, and exercises to help you develop and sustain this vital practice. Each chapter is designed to build upon the previous one, creating a comprehensive roadmap to self-discovery and self-acceptance.

- **Chapter 1: Understanding Self-Love** delves into the concept of self-love, dispelling common myths and highlighting its significance in our lives.
- **Chapter 2: The Journey Inward** guides you through the process of self-discovery, encouraging you to connect with your true self.
- **Chapter 3: Cultivating Self-Compassion** teaches you how to treat yourself with kindness and understanding, especially during challenging times.
- **Chapter 4: Building a Positive Self-Image** helps you develop a healthier perception of

yourself, counteracting negative self-talk and self-criticism.
- **Chapter 5: Nurturing Your Mind, Body, and Soul** provides holistic practices to care for your entire being, promoting overall well-being.
- **Chapter 6: Self-Love in Relationships** explores how self-love impacts and enhances your interactions with others, fostering healthier and more fulfilling connections.
- **Chapter 7: Living Authentically and Purposefully** encourages you to align your life with your true self and pursue your passions with intention.
- **Chapter 8: Sustaining Self-Love** offers strategies to maintain and deepen your self-love over the long term, ensuring it remains a guiding force in your life.

A Personal Commitment

Embarking on the journey of self-love requires a personal commitment. It's about choosing to prioritize yourself, to value your well-being, and to honor your needs and desires. This book is a companion on that journey, offering guidance, support, and encouragement along the way.

Remember, self-love is not about being selfish or narcissistic. It's about recognizing your inherent worth and treating yourself with the respect and kindness you deserve. It's about understanding that by loving yourself, you are better equipped to love and care for others.

Your Transformation Awaits

As you read through this book, I invite you to approach each chapter with an open heart and a willing spirit. Take your time with the exercises and reflections, allowing yourself to fully engage with the material. Be patient and gentle with yourself as you navigate this journey.

Unleashing the power of self-love can lead to profound changes in your life. It can help you break free from limiting beliefs, heal past wounds, and step into a more authentic and empowered version of yourself. It can enhance your relationships, boost your confidence, and bring greater joy and fulfillment into your daily life.

Are you ready to embark on this transformative journey? Together, let's unlock the power of self-love and discover the limitless potential within you.

"*Your journey to a more loving, compassionate, and empowered self begins now.*"

Chapter 1: Understanding Self-Love

What is Self-Love?

Self-love is the practice of valuing and caring for oneself. It involves recognizing your worth, treating yourself with kindness, and prioritizing your well-being. Far from being selfish or narcissistic, self-love is about acknowledging your inherent value and ensuring that your needs are met.

When you love yourself, you cultivate a deep sense of self-respect and self-compassion. This foundational practice influences your relationships, decision-making, and overall life satisfaction. Self-love empowers you to set healthy boundaries, pursue your passions, and live authentically.

Distinguishing Self-Love from Narcissism

One of the most common misconceptions about self-love is that it equates to narcissism. However, these two concepts are fundamentally different. Narcissism is characterized by an excessive focus on oneself, often at the expense of others. It involves a sense of superiority, entitlement, and a constant need for validation.

In contrast, self-love is rooted in humility and self-respect. It does not require comparison with others or external validation. Self-love is about recognizing your worth without diminishing the worth of others. It involves a healthy balance of self-care and empathy, allowing you to maintain strong, positive relationships.

The Impact of Self-Love on Mental Health and Well-Being

The benefits of self-love extend far beyond a positive self-image. Research has shown that self-love is closely linked to improved mental health and overall well-being. People who practice self-love tend to experience lower levels of stress, anxiety, and depression. They are more resilient in the face of challenges and are better equipped to cope with setbacks.

Self-love also promotes a positive outlook on life. When you love and accept yourself, you are more likely to pursue activities and relationships that bring you joy and fulfillment. This positive mindset can lead to a more satisfying and meaningful life.

The Myths and Misconceptions About Self-Love

Many myths and misconceptions surround the concept of self-love, often preventing people from embracing it fully. Let's explore some of these myths and debunk them:

Myth 1: Self-Love is Selfish

One of the most pervasive myths is that self-love is selfish. In reality, self-love is about recognizing your needs and ensuring they are met so that you can show up as your best self for others. When you take care of yourself, you are better equipped to care for those around you.

Myth 2: Self-Love is Narcissistic

As discussed earlier, self-love is not about feeling superior to others. It is about recognizing your worth and treating yourself with kindness and respect. Narcissism, on the other hand, involves an inflated sense of self-importance and a lack of empathy for others.

Myth 3: Self-Love is Indulgent

Some people believe that self-love involves excessive pampering or indulgence. While self-love can include activities like taking a relaxing bath or treating yourself to something special, it also involves setting boundaries, practicing self-compassion, and prioritizing your mental and emotional health.

Understanding Cultural and Societal Influences

Cultural and societal norms can significantly impact our perception of self-love. In many cultures, self-sacrifice and putting others first are highly valued, often at the expense of personal well-being. This can lead to feelings of guilt or shame when prioritizing self-love.

Societal influences, such as media and advertising, also play a role. We are constantly bombarded with images and messages that suggest we are not enough as we are. These messages can create unrealistic standards and contribute to feelings of inadequacy.

Understanding these influences is crucial in breaking free from negative thought patterns and embracing self-love. By recognizing the external factors that shape our self-perception, we can begin to challenge and change them.

The Science Behind Self-Love

Research in psychology and neuroscience supports the profound impact of self-love on our mental and physical health. Studies have shown that self-compassion, a key component of self-love, activates the brain's caregiving system, promoting feelings of safety and security.

Self-love practices, such as mindfulness and positive self-talk, have been linked to reduced levels of cortisol, the stress hormone. This can lead to lower levels of anxiety and depression, improved immune function, and better overall health.

Furthermore, self-love can enhance cognitive functioning. When we are not preoccupied with negative self-judgment, we have more mental energy available for creative thinking, problem-solving, and decision-making.

Practical Steps to Cultivate Self-Love

1. Practice Self-Compassion

- Be kind to yourself, especially during difficult times.
- Replace self-criticism with supportive and understanding self-talk.

2. Set Healthy Boundaries

- Learn to say no when necessary.
- Protect your time and energy by prioritizing activities and relationships that nourish you.

3. Prioritize Self-Care

- Make time for activities that bring you joy and relaxation.
- Pay attention to your physical, emotional, and mental health needs.

4. Embrace Your Authentic Self

- Accept yourself as you are, without trying to conform to external expectations.
- Celebrate your unique qualities and strengths.

5. Engage in Positive Self-Talk

- Challenge negative thoughts and replace them with affirming ones.
- Use affirmations to reinforce your self-worth and capabilities.

6. Surround Yourself with Supportive People

- Build relationships with people who uplift and support you.
- Distance yourself from those who drain your energy or undermine your self-esteem.

Understanding self-love is the first step towards a more fulfilling and authentic life. By recognizing the importance of self-love, debunking common myths, and understanding the science behind it, you can begin to cultivate a deeper sense of self-worth and compassion. This foundational practice will empower you to navigate life's challenges with resilience and grace, ultimately leading to a happier, healthier you.

Chapter 2: The Journey Inward

Self-Awareness as the First Step

Self-awareness is the cornerstone of self-love. It involves understanding your thoughts, emotions, and behaviors, and recognizing how they influence your interactions and experiences. By becoming more self-aware, you can identify patterns that may be holding you back and make conscious choices to change them.

Tools and Techniques for Self-Reflection

1. **Journaling:** Writing down your thoughts and feelings can help you gain clarity and insight. It allows you to track your emotional patterns and identify triggers.
2. **Mindfulness Meditation:** Practicing mindfulness helps you become more present and aware of your internal experiences. It involves paying attention to your thoughts and feelings without judgment.
3. **Self-Assessment Exercises:** Tools like personality tests, values assessments, and strengths inventories can provide valuable

insights into your unique qualities and preferences.
4. **Feedback from Others:** Asking trusted friends or family members for feedback can offer new perspectives and highlight blind spots in your self-awareness.

Identifying and Understanding Your Inner Critic

The inner critic is the voice inside your head that judges and criticizes you. It can be a significant barrier to self-love, often rooted in past experiences and negative self-beliefs. Understanding and addressing your inner critic is crucial for cultivating self-compassion.

1. **Recognize Your Inner Critic:** Pay attention to the negative thoughts and self-judgments that arise in your mind. Notice when and how they appear.
2. **Understand Its Origins:** Reflect on where your inner critic comes from. It may be influenced by past traumas, societal expectations, or early life experiences.
3. **Challenge Negative Thoughts:** When you notice self-critical thoughts, question their

validity. Are they based on facts, or are they exaggerated or irrational?
4. **Replace Criticism with Compassion:** Practice speaking to yourself with the same kindness and understanding you would offer a friend. Use affirmations and positive self-talk to counteract negative thoughts.

Embracing Your True Self

Embracing your true self means accepting and celebrating who you are, without trying to conform to external expectations. It involves recognizing your strengths and weaknesses, and understanding that you are worthy of love and respect just as you are.

The Importance of Authenticity

Living authentically means aligning your actions and choices with your true self. It involves being honest about your needs, desires, and values, and expressing them openly. Authenticity fosters deeper connections with others and allows you to live a more fulfilling and meaningful life.

Exercises to Connect with Your True Self

1. **Values Clarification:** Identify your core values and consider how they influence your decisions and actions. Reflect on whether you are living in alignment with these values.
2. **Strengths Identification:** Recognize your unique strengths and talents. Consider how you can leverage them in your personal and professional life.
3. **Passion Exploration:** Reflect on activities and pursuits that bring you joy and fulfillment. Make time for these passions in your daily life.
4. **Visualization:** Imagine a life where you are living authentically and fully embracing your true self. Visualize the steps needed to achieve this vision.

Healing from Past Wounds

Emotional healing is a crucial part of the journey inward. It involves acknowledging and processing past traumas and letting go of the pain and resentment that may be holding you back.

Acknowledging and Processing Past Traumas

1. **Identify Your Wounds:** Reflect on past experiences that have caused you pain or trauma. Acknowledge the impact they have had on your life.
2. **Allow Yourself to Feel:** Give yourself permission to feel the emotions associated with these experiences. Suppressing emotions can hinder the healing process.
3. **Seek Professional Support:** Consider working with a therapist or counselor to help you process and heal from past traumas.
4. **Practice Self-Compassion:** Be gentle with yourself as you navigate the healing process. Understand that healing takes time and patience.

Techniques for Emotional Healing and Forgiveness

1. **Mindfulness and Meditation:** Practices like mindfulness and meditation can help you stay present and process difficult emotions.
2. **Forgiveness Practices:** Forgiveness is not about condoning harmful behavior, but about releasing the hold that past hurts have

on you. Consider forgiveness exercises, such as writing a letter to the person who hurt you (even if you don't send it).
3. **Creative Expression:** Art, music, writing, and other forms of creative expression can be powerful tools for emotional healing. They allow you to process and release emotions in a constructive way.
4. **Self-Care:** Prioritize self-care activities that nurture your body, mind, and soul. This can include physical exercise, relaxation techniques, and spending time in nature.

The journey inward is a transformative process that lays the foundation for true self-love. By becoming more self-aware, embracing your authentic self, and healing from past wounds, you create the space for deeper self-compassion and acceptance. This inner work is essential for cultivating a life of fulfillment, joy, and meaningful connection with yourself and others. Embrace this journey with an open heart, and you will discover the profound power of self-love.

Chapter 3: Cultivating Self-Compassion

Understanding Self-Compassion

Self-compassion is the practice of treating yourself with the same kindness, care, and understanding that you would offer to a friend. It involves recognizing your own suffering, acknowledging that it is a shared human experience, and responding with empathy and support rather than judgment and criticism.

Definition and Benefits

Self-compassion consists of three key components:

1. **Self-Kindness:** Being warm and understanding towards yourself during times of pain or failure, rather than being harshly self-critical.
2. **Common Humanity:** Recognizing that suffering and personal inadequacy are part of the shared human experience. This awareness helps you feel connected to others rather than isolated.

3. **Mindfulness:** Holding your painful thoughts and feelings in balanced awareness, rather than over-identifying with them. This means acknowledging your suffering without being consumed by it.

The benefits of self-compassion are profound. Research shows that self-compassion is associated with greater emotional resilience, reduced stress and anxiety, higher levels of happiness, and more satisfying relationships. It allows you to navigate life's challenges with greater ease and fosters a more positive and balanced self-view.

The Difference Between Self-Compassion and Self-Pity

While self-compassion involves a healthy recognition of and response to your own suffering, self-pity tends to involve a sense of victimhood and isolation. Self-pity can amplify negative emotions and make you feel stuck, whereas self-compassion encourages growth and healing. By cultivating self-compassion, you can approach your difficulties with a constructive and supportive mindset.

Practices for Developing Self-Compassion

Cultivating self-compassion requires practice and intention. Here are some effective practices to help you develop this crucial skill:

Mindfulness and Meditation

Mindfulness meditation is a powerful tool for developing self-compassion. It involves paying attention to the present moment with a non-judgmental and accepting attitude. Here are a few mindfulness practices to try:

1. **Loving-Kindness Meditation:** This practice involves silently repeating phrases that convey good wishes towards yourself and others. For example: "May I be happy. May I be healthy. May I be safe. May I live with ease." Extend these wishes to others as well.
2. **Self-Compassion Break:** When you are experiencing a difficult moment, pause and acknowledge your suffering. Place your hand on your heart and repeat phrases such as: "This is a moment of suffering. Suffering is part of life. May I be kind to myself in this moment."

3. **Mindful Breathing:** Focus on your breath as it flows in and out. If your mind wanders, gently bring your attention back to your breath. This practice helps you stay present and reduces over-identification with negative thoughts.

Self-Compassion Exercises and Affirmations

1. **Write a Self-Compassionate Letter:** Write a letter to yourself from the perspective of a compassionate friend. Acknowledge your struggles and offer words of kindness and support. Read the letter whenever you need a boost of self-compassion.
2. **Positive Affirmations:** Create a list of affirmations that resonate with you and repeat them daily. Examples include: "I am worthy of love and kindness," "I am doing my best," and "I am enough just as I am."
3. **Compassionate Touch:** Physical gestures of self-compassion, such as placing a hand over your heart or giving yourself a hug, can be soothing and grounding. These actions activate the body's caregiving system, promoting feelings of safety and comfort.

Overcoming Obstacles to Self-Compassion

Cultivating self-compassion can be challenging, especially if you are accustomed to self-criticism or have internalized negative beliefs about yourself. Here are some strategies to help you overcome common obstacles:

Dealing with Guilt and Shame

Guilt and shame can be significant barriers to self-compassion. Guilt is the feeling of having done something wrong, while shame is the feeling of being inherently flawed. To overcome these emotions:

1. **Acknowledge Your Feelings:** Allow yourself to feel and express your guilt and shame without judgment. Recognize that these emotions are a natural part of the human experience.
2. **Challenge Negative Beliefs:** Identify the beliefs underlying your guilt and shame. Are they realistic or fair? Replace them with more balanced and compassionate thoughts.
3. **Seek Support:** Talk to a trusted friend, therapist, or support group about your

feelings. Sharing your experiences can help you feel less isolated and more understood.

Building Resilience

Resilience is the ability to bounce back from adversity. Self-compassion can enhance your resilience by providing emotional support and reducing self-blame. Here are some ways to build resilience through self-compassion:

1. **Practice Gratitude:** Focus on the positive aspects of your life and express gratitude for them. This practice can shift your perspective and increase your emotional resilience.
2. **Develop a Growth Mindset:** Embrace challenges as opportunities for growth and learning. Understand that mistakes and failures are part of the journey, not reflections of your worth.
3. **Nurture Relationships:** Build and maintain supportive relationships with others. Social connections can provide a buffer against stress and enhance your overall well-being.

Cultivating self-compassion is a transformative practice that can profoundly impact your relationship with yourself and others. By understanding self-compassion, practicing mindfulness and self-care, and overcoming obstacles, you can develop a kinder, more supportive inner voice. This shift will allow you to navigate life's challenges with greater ease and grace, ultimately leading to a more fulfilling and compassionate existence. Embrace the journey of self-compassion, and you will unlock the power to heal, grow, and thrive.

Chapter 4: Building a Positive Self-Image

The Power of Positive Self-Talk

Our internal dialogue significantly shapes our self-image and overall well-being. Positive self-talk involves intentionally focusing on affirming and encouraging thoughts, which can help replace negative patterns that undermine our confidence and self-worth.

Replacing Negative Thoughts with Positive Affirmations

Negative thoughts often arise from deep-seated beliefs about ourselves. To counteract these, we can practice the following steps:

1. **Identify Negative Thoughts:** Pay attention to your internal dialogue and note when negative thoughts occur. These might include thoughts like "I'm not good enough," "I always fail," or "I don't deserve happiness."
2. **Challenge the Validity:** Question whether these thoughts are true or helpful. Are they

based on facts, or are they irrational and unproductive?
3. **Replace with Positive Affirmations:** Create a list of positive affirmations that resonate with you. For example, "I am capable and strong," "I learn and grow from every experience," or "I am deserving of love and respect." Repeat these affirmations regularly to reinforce a positive self-image.

Techniques for Rewiring Your Brain

The brain is adaptable and capable of forming new neural pathways—a concept known as neuroplasticity. By consistently practicing positive self-talk and affirmations, you can rewire your brain to default to more supportive and empowering thoughts. Here are some techniques:

1. **Daily Affirmations:** Start and end your day with positive affirmations. Write them down, say them aloud, or repeat them in your mind.
2. **Visualization:** Imagine yourself achieving your goals and embodying your desired qualities. Visualization helps to create a mental image of success and reinforces positive beliefs.

3. **Gratitude Practice:** Regularly reflect on what you are grateful for. This practice shifts your focus from what you lack to what you have, fostering a more positive outlook.
4. **Surround Yourself with Positivity:** Engage with people, media, and activities that uplift and inspire you. Positive environments reinforce positive thinking.

Body Positivity and Acceptance

A significant aspect of building a positive self-image involves accepting and appreciating your physical self. Body positivity is about recognizing and respecting the diversity of body shapes and sizes, and understanding that all bodies are worthy of love and care.

Embracing Your Physical Self

1. **Practice Self-Acceptance:** Acknowledge your body as it is right now, without judgment. Understand that your worth is not determined by your appearance.
2. **Focus on Functionality:** Appreciate what your body can do rather than how it looks. Celebrate your body's abilities, such as strength, flexibility, and endurance.

3. **Challenge Unrealistic Standards:** Recognize that societal standards of beauty are often unrealistic and unattainable. Embrace your unique features and resist comparisons with others.

Practices for Body Positivity

1. **Mindful Movement:** Engage in physical activities that you enjoy and that make you feel good. Focus on the pleasure and benefits of movement rather than on achieving a certain appearance.
2. **Nourishing Your Body:** Eat in a way that fuels and nourishes your body. Pay attention to how different foods make you feel, and prioritize those that contribute to your well-being.
3. **Positive Body Talk:** Speak kindly to and about your body. Avoid negative comments about your appearance and practice complimenting yourself on qualities beyond your looks.
4. **Body-Positive Media:** Consume media that promotes diverse and realistic representations of bodies. Follow social media accounts and read content that uplift and inspire body positivity.

Setting Healthy Boundaries

Healthy boundaries are essential for maintaining a positive self-image and protecting your mental and emotional well-being. Boundaries help you define what is acceptable and unacceptable behavior from others and ensure that your needs are respected.

Understanding the Importance of Boundaries

Boundaries are crucial for several reasons:

1. **Self-Respect:** Setting boundaries communicates to yourself and others that you value and respect your own needs and limits.
2. **Emotional Protection:** Boundaries help protect you from emotional harm and prevent you from feeling overwhelmed or taken advantage of.
3. **Healthy Relationships:** Clear boundaries contribute to healthier and more respectful relationships by fostering mutual respect and understanding.

Techniques for Setting and Maintaining Boundaries

1. **Identify Your Needs:** Reflect on what is important to you and what you need to feel safe, respected, and valued. This may include emotional, physical, and time boundaries.
2. **Communicate Clearly:** Express your boundaries assertively and respectfully. Use "I" statements to communicate your needs without blaming or criticizing others. For example, "I need some alone time to recharge after work."
3. **Be Consistent:** Consistency is key to maintaining boundaries. Enforce your boundaries consistently to reinforce their importance and prevent others from overstepping them.
4. **Practice Self-Care:** Setting boundaries can be challenging, especially if you are not used to it. Practice self-care to support yourself through the process, and seek support from friends, family, or a therapist if needed.

Building a positive self-image is a multifaceted journey that involves cultivating positive self-talk, embracing body positivity, and setting healthy boundaries. By intentionally replacing negative thoughts with affirming ones, accepting and appreciating your physical self, and protecting your well-being through clear boundaries, you can develop a more empowering and nurturing relationship with yourself. This positive self-image will not only enhance your self-love but also improve your overall quality of life, enabling you to navigate the world with confidence and joy.

Chapter 5: Nurturing Your Mind, Body, and Soul

The Holistic Approach to Self-Care

Nurturing yourself involves taking a holistic approach to self-care, which means caring for your mind, body, and soul. This comprehensive approach ensures that you are addressing all aspects of your well-being, leading to a more balanced and fulfilling life.

Mind-Body Connection

The mind-body connection emphasizes the interdependence of mental and physical health. Stress, for instance, can manifest physically as headaches or muscle tension, while physical activity can improve mood and cognitive function. Recognizing and nurturing this connection is essential for holistic well-being.

Holistic Self-Care Practices

1. **Mindfulness and Meditation:** These practices help you stay present, reduce stress, and enhance mental clarity. Regular

meditation can improve emotional regulation and overall mental health.
2. **Physical Activity:** Exercise is vital for physical health and also releases endorphins that boost mood. Find activities you enjoy, whether it's yoga, dancing, running, or walking.
3. **Nutrition:** Eating a balanced diet rich in nutrients fuels your body and mind. Pay attention to how different foods affect your energy levels and mood.
4. **Rest and Sleep:** Quality sleep is crucial for mental and physical health. Establish a regular sleep routine and create a restful environment to ensure you get 7 to 8 hours of adequate rest.

Mental Health and Emotional Well-Being

Taking care of your mental health is a key component of nurturing your overall well-being. It involves managing stress, processing emotions, and seeking help when needed.

Managing Stress

1. **Identify Stressors:** Recognize the sources of your stress. This awareness can help you address and manage them more effectively.
2. **Relaxation Techniques:** Practices like deep breathing, progressive muscle relaxation, and guided imagery can help reduce stress and promote relaxation.
3. **Time Management:** Prioritize tasks and set realistic goals to prevent feeling overwhelmed. Break tasks into manageable steps and take breaks when needed.

Processing Emotions

1. **Acknowledge Your Feelings:** Allow yourself to feel and express your emotions without judgment. Suppressing emotions can lead to increased stress and anxiety.
2. **Emotional Expression:** Find healthy ways to express your emotions, such as talking to a friend, journaling, or engaging in creative activities.
3. **Mindful Awareness:** Practice mindfulness to observe your emotions without getting caught up in them. This can help you

respond to your feelings in a balanced and constructive way.

Seeking Support

1. **Therapy and Counseling:** Professional support can provide valuable insights and coping strategies for managing mental health challenges.
2. **Support Networks:** Build a network of supportive friends and family members who can offer understanding and encouragement.
3. **Self-Help Resources:** Books, online courses, and support groups can also provide tools and guidance for improving mental health.

Physical Health and Vitality

Caring for your body involves more than just exercise and nutrition. It encompasses all aspects of physical well-being, including rest, hydration, and listening to your body's signals.

Exercise and Movement

1. **Find Enjoyable Activities:** Choose physical activities that you enjoy to make exercise a regular and enjoyable part of your routine.
2. **Incorporate Variety:** Mix different types of exercise, such as cardio, strength training, and flexibility exercises, to keep your routine balanced and interesting.
3. **Set Realistic Goals:** Set achievable fitness goals and celebrate your progress, no matter how small.

Nutrition and Hydration

1. **Balanced Diet:** Eat a variety of foods that provide essential nutrients. Include fruits, vegetables, whole grains, lean proteins, and healthy fats in your diet.
2. **Hydration:** Drink plenty of water throughout the day to stay hydrated and support your body's functions.
3. **Mindful Eating:** Pay attention to your hunger and fullness cues, and choose foods that nourish your body and mind.

Rest and Recovery

1. **Sleep Hygiene:** Establish a regular sleep schedule and create a calming bedtime routine. Avoid screens and caffeine before bed to improve sleep quality.
2. **Rest Days:** Allow your body time to rest and recover, especially after intense physical activity.
3. **Listen to Your Body:** Pay attention to signs of fatigue or illness and give yourself permission to rest when needed.

Spiritual Health and Inner Peace

Nurturing your soul involves connecting with your inner self, finding meaning and purpose, and fostering a sense of inner peace. Spiritual health is unique to each individual and can be nurtured through various practices.

Finding Meaning and Purpose

1. **Reflect on Values and Beliefs:** Spend time contemplating your core values and beliefs. Understanding what matters most to you can guide your actions and decisions.

2. **Set Meaningful Goals:** Align your goals with your values and pursue activities that bring you fulfillment and joy.
3. **Volunteer and Give Back:** Helping others can provide a sense of purpose and connection to something larger than yourself.

Practices for Inner Peace

1. **Meditation and Prayer:** Regular meditation or prayer can foster a sense of connection and tranquility.
2. **Nature Connection:** Spend time in nature to recharge and find peace. Activities like hiking, gardening, or simply sitting outdoors can be restorative.
3. **Creative Expression:** Engage in creative activities that allow you to express yourself and connect with your inner self, such as writing, painting, or playing music.

Nurturing your mind, body, and soul is essential for holistic well-being. By adopting a comprehensive approach to self-care that addresses mental health, physical vitality, and spiritual health, you can create a balanced and fulfilling life. Embrace practices that resonate with you and make self-care a priority, understanding that nurturing yourself is a continuous journey of growth and self-love. This commitment to your well-being will enhance your ability to live authentically, cope with challenges, and experience greater joy and satisfaction in life.

Chapter 6: Self-Love in Relationships

The Foundation of Healthy Relationships

Self-love is the cornerstone of healthy, fulfilling relationships. When you have a strong sense of self-love, you bring authenticity, confidence, and emotional stability to your interactions with others. This chapter explores how self-love influences your relationships and provides practical strategies for nurturing self-love within the context of your connections with others.

The Role of Self-Love in Relationships

1. **Self-Worth:** When you value and love yourself, you set the standard for how others should treat you. You recognize your worth and are less likely to tolerate disrespect or unhealthy behavior.
2. **Boundaries:** Self-love empowers you to establish and maintain healthy boundaries, ensuring that your needs and well-being are prioritized.
3. **Authenticity:** Loving yourself allows you to show up authentically in relationships,

fostering genuine connections based on mutual respect and understanding.
4. **Emotional Resilience:** A strong sense of self-love provides a solid emotional foundation, helping you navigate conflicts and challenges in relationships with greater ease.

Building Self-Love in Romantic Relationships

Romantic relationships can be a powerful arena for practicing and deepening self-love. Here are some ways to cultivate self-love within your romantic connections:

Maintaining Your Individuality

1. **Personal Interests:** Continue pursuing your hobbies and interests, even when in a relationship. This nurtures your sense of self and prevents you from losing your identity.
2. **Alone Time:** Ensure you have regular alone time to recharge and connect with yourself. This helps maintain a healthy balance between togetherness and independence.
3. **Self-Reflection:** Regularly reflect on your personal growth and goals. This practice

keeps you grounded in your own journey and helps you remain true to yourself.

Communicating Your Needs

1. **Assertive Communication:** Express your needs and desires clearly and respectfully. Assertive communication fosters understanding and ensures that your needs are met.
2. **Active Listening:** Practice active listening with your partner, showing empathy and understanding. This creates a supportive environment where both partners feel heard and valued.
3. **Mutual Support:** Encourage a dynamic of mutual support, where both partners are committed to each other's well-being and growth.

Addressing Self-Sabotage

1. **Recognize Patterns:** Identify patterns of self-sabotage, such as negative self-talk, fear of vulnerability, or pushing your partner away. Awareness is the first step to change.
2. **Challenge Negative Beliefs:** Work on challenging and reframing negative beliefs

about yourself and your worthiness of love. Replace them with affirming and empowering thoughts.
3. **Seek Professional Help:** Consider seeking therapy or counseling to address deep-seated issues that may be affecting your relationships. Professional support can provide valuable tools and insights for healing and growth.

Cultivating Self-Love in Friendships

Friendships are another vital aspect of our lives where self-love plays a crucial role. Here's how to nurture self-love within your friendships:

Choosing Healthy Friendships

1. **Positive Influences:** Surround yourself with friends who uplift, inspire, and support you. Choose friendships that are based on mutual respect and shared values.
2. **Letting Go of Toxicity:** Recognize when a friendship is toxic or draining. It's okay to distance yourself or end relationships that negatively impact your well-being.

Practicing Self-Respect

1. **Speak Your Truth:** Be honest and authentic in your friendships. Communicate openly about your feelings, thoughts, and boundaries.
2. **Stand Up for Yourself:** Don't be afraid to stand up for yourself if a friend is disrespectful or crosses your boundaries. Assertive communication is key to maintaining self-respect.
3. **Value Reciprocity:** Friendships should be reciprocal, with both parties giving and receiving support. Ensure that your friendships are balanced and mutually beneficial.

Supporting Each Other's Growth

1. **Celebrate Successes:** Celebrate each other's achievements and milestones. Genuine joy for your friends' successes strengthens your bond and promotes a positive dynamic.
2. **Encourage Growth:** Encourage your friends to pursue their passions and personal growth. Be a source of support and inspiration for each other.

3. **Practice Empathy:** Show empathy and understanding during difficult times. Being there for your friends, while also taking care of your own needs, fosters a supportive and nurturing friendship.

Enhancing Self-Love in Family Relationships

Family relationships can be complex and deeply rooted, making self-love both challenging and essential. Here's how to enhance self-love within your family dynamics:

Navigating Family Expectations

1. **Set Boundaries:** Establish clear boundaries with family members, especially if their expectations or behaviors are detrimental to your well-being.
2. **Communicate Needs:** Communicate your needs and boundaries assertively and respectfully. This can help reduce misunderstandings and conflicts.
3. **Seek Understanding:** Strive to understand your family members' perspectives and motivations, even if you don't agree with

them. This can foster compassion and reduce tension.

Healing Family Wounds

1. **Acknowledge Pain:** Recognize and acknowledge any pain or trauma caused by family dynamics. Suppressing these emotions can hinder your self-love journey.
2. **Seek Professional Help:** Consider therapy or counseling to work through family-related issues. A professional can help you navigate complex emotions and develop healthy coping strategies.
3. **Practice Forgiveness:** Forgiveness is a powerful tool for healing. Forgiving doesn't mean condoning harmful behavior but rather freeing yourself from the burden of resentment.

Fostering Healthy Family Relationships

1. **Mutual Respect:** Foster a culture of mutual respect within your family. Respect each other's boundaries, choices, and individuality.

2. **Quality Time:** Spend quality time with your family, engaging in activities that strengthen your bond and create positive memories.
3. **Model Self-Love:** Be a role model of self-love for your family. Demonstrating self-care, self-respect, and healthy boundaries can inspire others to do the same.

Self-love is integral to creating and maintaining healthy, fulfilling relationships. By valuing yourself, setting boundaries, and communicating openly, you can nurture self-love within your romantic relationships, friendships, and family dynamics. This foundation of self-love not only enhances your relationships but also enriches your overall well-being, enabling you to connect more deeply and authentically with others. Embrace the journey of self-love in your relationships, and experience the transformative power of loving yourself and those around you.

Chapter 7: Living Authentically and Purposefully

The Essence of Authenticity

Living authentically means embracing and expressing your true self in all areas of your life. It involves being genuine, transparent, and aligned with your values and beliefs. Authenticity allows you to build a life that reflects who you truly are, fostering deeper connections and a greater sense of fulfillment.

Understanding Authenticity

1. **Self-Awareness:** Authenticity begins with self-awareness. This involves understanding your values, beliefs, strengths, and weaknesses.
2. **Consistency:** Living authentically means being consistent in your thoughts, words, and actions. It's about showing up as your true self in all situations.
3. **Vulnerability:** Authenticity requires vulnerability. It's about being open and honest, even when it feels uncomfortable or risky.

Barriers to Authenticity

1. **Fear of Judgment:** The fear of being judged or rejected by others can hinder authenticity. Overcoming this fear involves building self-confidence and self-acceptance.
2. **Social Pressure:** Societal norms and expectations can pressure you to conform. Recognizing and resisting these pressures is crucial for living authentically.
3. **Internal Critic:** Your inner critic can undermine your efforts to be authentic. Practice self-compassion and challenge negative self-talk to quiet this inner voice.

The Power of Purpose

Living purposefully means aligning your actions with your values and passions. It involves pursuing meaningful goals that resonate with your true self, leading to a more satisfying and impactful life.

Identifying Your Purpose

1. **Reflect on Passions:** Consider what activities and topics ignite your passion.

These interests often provide clues to your purpose.
2. **Assess Strengths:** Identify your strengths and talents. How can you use these abilities to contribute to something meaningful?
3. **Clarify Values:** Define your core values. What principles guide your decisions and actions? Aligning with your values is key to finding purpose.

Living with Purpose

1. **Set Meaningful Goals:** Establish goals that align with your purpose and values. These goals should inspire and motivate you.
2. **Take Action:** Purpose requires action. Break down your goals into actionable steps and commit to making progress.
3. **Embrace Challenges:** Pursuing your purpose may involve challenges and setbacks. View these as opportunities for growth and learning.

Integrating Authenticity and Purpose

Living authentically and purposefully involves harmonizing your true self with your life's mission.

Here's how to integrate these concepts into your daily life:

Aligning Actions with Values

1. **Daily Reflection:** Reflect on your actions daily. Are they aligned with your values and purpose? Adjust your behavior as needed.
2. **Intentional Living:** Make conscious choices that reflect your true self. Be mindful of your decisions and their alignment with your values.
3. **Authentic Relationships:** Build relationships that support and encourage your authenticity and purpose. Surround yourself with people who uplift and inspire you.

Balancing Authenticity and Adaptability

1. **Stay True to Yourself:** While being adaptable is important, don't compromise your core values and beliefs. Find a balance that allows you to be flexible without losing your authenticity.
2. **Embrace Change:** Be open to growth and change. Authenticity is not about being rigid

but about evolving in a way that remains true to your core self.
3. **Continuous Learning:** Commit to continuous learning and self-improvement. Seek out experiences and knowledge that help you grow and stay aligned with your purpose.

Practical Strategies for Living Authentically and Purposefully

1. **Journaling:** Regular journaling can help you reflect on your values, goals, and experiences. It's a tool for self-discovery and alignment.
2. **Mindfulness Practices:** Mindfulness helps you stay present and connected to your true self. Practices like meditation and deep breathing can enhance self-awareness.
3. **Vision Boards:** Create a vision board that represents your goals and values. Visual reminders can keep you focused and motivated.
4. **Accountability Partners:** Find a trusted friend or mentor who can support you in your journey. Share your goals and progress with them for accountability.

Overcoming Challenges on the Path

Living authentically and purposefully is not always easy. Here are some common challenges and ways to overcome them:

Fear of Failure

1. **Redefine Failure:** View failure as a learning opportunity rather than a setback. Every failure is a step towards growth and success.
2. **Take Risks:** Embrace calculated risks. Stepping out of your comfort zone is essential for achieving your goals.
3. **Celebrate Efforts:** Celebrate your efforts and progress, regardless of the outcome. Recognize the courage it takes to pursue your purpose.

External Expectations

1. **Set Boundaries:** Set boundaries with people who try to impose their expectations on you. Communicate your needs and values clearly.
2. **Seek Support:** Surround yourself with supportive individuals who respect and encourage your authenticity.

3. **Trust Yourself:** Trust your intuition and judgment. You know what's best for you better than anyone else.

Internal Doubts

1. **Practice Self-Compassion:** Treat yourself with kindness and understanding. Everyone has doubts; it's how you handle them that matters.
2. **Affirmations:** Use positive affirmations to reinforce your confidence and self-belief. Remind yourself of your strengths and capabilities.
3. **Reflect on Achievements:** Regularly reflect on your past achievements and successes. This can boost your confidence and remind you of your potential.

Living authentically and purposefully is a transformative journey that leads to greater fulfillment and happiness. By embracing your true self, aligning your actions with your values, and pursuing meaningful goals, you can create a life that reflects who you truly are. This journey requires courage, self-compassion, and resilience, but the rewards are profound. Embrace the path of authenticity and purpose, and experience the joy and satisfaction of living a life true to yourself.

Chapter 8: Sustaining Self-Love

The Continuous Journey of Self-Love

Self-love is not a destination but an ongoing journey. It requires consistent effort, awareness, and dedication. Just as any other relationship, the one you have with yourself needs regular nurturing to remain strong and healthy. This chapter explores practical strategies for sustaining self-love over the long term, ensuring it remains a guiding force in your life.

Daily Practices for Self-Love

Incorporating self-love into your daily routine can help reinforce its presence in your life. Here are some practical daily practices:

Morning Rituals

1. **Affirmations:** Start your day with positive affirmations. Statements like "I am worthy," "I am enough," and "I love and accept myself" can set a positive tone for the day.
2. **Gratitude Practice:** Spend a few minutes each morning reflecting on what you are

grateful for. This practice can shift your focus to the positive aspects of your life and foster a sense of appreciation.
3. **Mindful Moments:** Begin your day with mindfulness exercises such as deep breathing or meditation. These practices can center your mind and enhance your awareness of your thoughts and feelings.

Self-Care Activities

1. **Physical Activity:** Regular exercise is crucial for both physical and mental well-being. Find activities you enjoy and make them a regular part of your routine.
2. **Nourishing Nutrition:** Pay attention to your diet, ensuring it is balanced and nutritious. Nourishing your body is a fundamental act of self-love.
3. **Rest and Relaxation:** Prioritize rest and relaxation. Ensure you get enough sleep and take breaks throughout the day to recharge.

Evening Reflections

1. **Journaling:** Reflect on your day through journaling. Write about your experiences, emotions, and any lessons learned. This

practice can help you process your thoughts and reinforce self-awareness.
2. **Self-Compassion:** Before bed, practice self-compassion. Reflect on any challenges you faced and acknowledge your efforts. Remind yourself that it's okay to make mistakes and that you are deserving of kindness and understanding.
3. **Relaxation Rituals:** Develop a calming evening routine that promotes relaxation. This might include reading, taking a warm bath, or listening to soothing music.

Building a Supportive Environment

Your environment plays a significant role in sustaining self-love. Surround yourself with people and influences that support and uplift you.

Positive Relationships

1. **Supportive Friends:** Cultivate friendships with people who encourage and inspire you. These relationships should be based on mutual respect and understanding.
2. **Boundaries:** Set and maintain healthy boundaries in your relationships. Protect

your emotional and mental well-being by ensuring your needs are respected.
3. **Seek Encouragement:** Don't hesitate to seek encouragement and support from your loved ones. Sharing your journey with others can provide motivation and reassurance.

Inspirational Resources

1. **Books and Articles:** Read books and articles that inspire and educate you about self-love. Learning from others' experiences and insights can provide valuable guidance.
2. **Podcasts and Videos:** Listen to podcasts or watch videos that promote self-love and personal growth. These resources can offer practical tips and motivation.
3. **Affirmative Spaces:** Create physical spaces in your home that promote positivity and relaxation. Surround yourself with items that bring you joy and comfort.

Self-Reflection and Growth

Sustaining self-love requires ongoing self-reflection and a commitment to personal growth. Regularly assessing your journey and making necessary adjustments can help maintain your self-love.

Regular Self-Assessments

1. **Check-Ins:** Schedule regular self-check-ins to evaluate your emotional and mental state. Ask yourself how you are feeling and what you need to support your well-being.
2. **Progress Tracking:** Keep track of your progress in your self-love journey. Celebrate your achievements and identify areas for improvement.
3. **Goal Setting:** Set new goals that align with your growth and development. These goals should be realistic and meaningful to you.

Embracing Change

1. **Flexibility:** Be open to change and adaptability. Life is dynamic, and your self-love practices should evolve with your experiences and circumstances.
2. **Learning Mindset:** Adopt a learning mindset. View challenges and setbacks as opportunities for growth and learning.
3. **Self-Compassion:** Practice self-compassion when facing change. Understand that growth

can be uncomfortable and that it's okay to take things one step at a time.

Overcoming Obstacles

Challenges and obstacles are inevitable in any journey. Here are some strategies to overcome obstacles to sustaining self-love:

Dealing with Negative Self-Talk

1. **Identify Triggers:** Recognize situations or thoughts that trigger negative self-talk. Awareness is the first step to addressing them.
2. **Reframe Thoughts:** Challenge and reframe negative thoughts into positive or neutral ones. Focus on your strengths and accomplishments.
3. **Affirmations:** Use positive affirmations to counteract negative self-talk. Remind yourself of your worth and capabilities.

Managing Stress and Anxiety

1. **Stress Management Techniques:** Practice stress management techniques such as deep breathing, meditation, or yoga. These

practices can help reduce anxiety and promote relaxation.
2. **Time Management:** Organize your time effectively to prevent overwhelm. Prioritize tasks and allow time for self-care and relaxation.
3. **Seek Support:** If stress and anxiety become overwhelming, seek support from friends, family, or a mental health professional.

Handling Setbacks

1. **Acceptance:** Accept that setbacks are a part of the journey. They do not define your worth or progress.
2. **Learn and Adapt:** Learn from setbacks and adapt your strategies. Use these experiences as opportunities for growth and improvement.
3. **Persistence:** Stay committed to your self-love journey. Persistence and resilience are key to overcoming obstacles and sustaining self-love.

Sustaining self-love is an ongoing commitment that requires daily practices, a supportive environment, self-reflection, and resilience. By incorporating self-love into your routine, building positive relationships, embracing change, and overcoming obstacles, you can maintain and deepen your self-love over time. Remember that self-love is a journey, not a destination, and each step you take towards nurturing yourself contributes to a more fulfilling and authentic life. Embrace the continuous journey of self-love and allow it to guide you towards greater happiness and well-being.

Conclusion: Unleashing the Power of Self-Love

Unleashing the power of self-love is a transformative journey that touches every aspect of your life. Throughout this book, we have explored the foundational principles and practical strategies for understanding, cultivating, and sustaining self-love. Now, as we conclude, it's essential to reflect on the overarching themes and the profound impact that self-love can have on your life.

Embracing Your True Self

Self-love begins with self-awareness and acceptance. By embracing your true self—acknowledging your strengths, weaknesses, and unique qualities—you lay the groundwork for a life filled with authenticity and purpose. Remember that self-love is not about perfection; it's about accepting yourself as you are and celebrating your individuality.

Building a Strong Foundation

Self-love serves as the foundation for healthy relationships, emotional resilience, and personal growth. It empowers you to set and maintain boundaries, pursue your passions, and live in alignment with your values. By prioritizing self-love, you create a stable and nurturing environment in which you can thrive.

Cultivating Compassion and Kindness

Self-love involves treating yourself with the same compassion and kindness that you would offer to a loved one. It requires forgiving yourself for past mistakes, being patient with your growth, and showing yourself empathy during challenging times. Through self-compassion, you build a reservoir of inner strength and resilience.

Living Authentically and Purposefully

Authenticity and purpose are central to a fulfilling life. By living authentically, you honor your true self and foster genuine connections with others. Pursuing a life of purpose involves aligning your actions with your values and passions, creating a sense of meaning and direction. Together, authenticity and purpose lead to a life that feels rich and rewarding.

Sustaining Self-Love

Sustaining self-love is an ongoing process that requires consistent effort and dedication. Incorporating daily practices, building a supportive environment, and committing to continuous growth are essential for maintaining self-love over the long term. Remember that self-love is a journey, not a destination, and each day offers new opportunities for nurturing and deepening your relationship with yourself.

The Ripple Effect of Self-Love

The power of self-love extends beyond your own well-being. When you love and care for yourself, you radiate positivity and strength, influencing those around you. Your relationships become healthier, your interactions more meaningful, and your contributions to the world more impactful. Self-love creates a ripple effect, spreading love and positivity far and wide.

Your Journey Ahead

As you move forward, carry the lessons and insights from this book with you. Embrace the journey of self-love with an open heart and a curious mind. Be patient with yourself, celebrate your progress, and stay committed to your growth. Remember that self-love is the key to unlocking your full potential and living a life that is true to who you are.

Unleashing the power of self-love transforms not only your inner world but also the world around you. It empowers you to live authentically, pursue your passions, and build meaningful relationships. By prioritizing self-love, you create a life that is rich in joy, purpose, and fulfillment.

May your journey of self-love be filled with discovery, growth, and boundless love. Embrace the power within you, and let it guide you towards a life of profound happiness and fulfillment.

www.ingramcontent.com/pod-product-compliance
Lightning Source LLC
LaVergne TN
LVHW061048070526
838201LV00074B/5223